Happily Grateful

"We can only be said to be alive in those moments," writes Thornton Wilder, "when our hearts are conscious of our treasure."

This is the gift—to hear and enjoy life's music everywhere. To be more aware of what we have than what we don't have. To appreciate again and again all the wonderful things life has to offer us. Because there is truly something to celebrate every day.

And once we find that gift, it will stay with us and become a wellspring of joy. As the days go by and the moments we celebrate add up, our hearts will fill with riches, and we will be happily grateful.

The most precious things
of life are near at hand...

John Burroughs

Today a new sun rises for me;
everything lives, everything is animated,
everything seems to speak to me of my
passion, everything invites me to cherish it.

Anne de Lenclos

Each day comes to me with
both hands full of possibilities...

Helen Keller

Welcome the good that each day brings.

...look at everything always as though you were seeing it either for the first or last time...

Betty Smith

The most fortunate are those who have
a wonderful capacity to appreciate again and
again, freshly and naively, the basic goods of life,
with awe, pleasure, wonder, and even ecstasy.

Abraham Maslow

Stop every now and then. Just stop
and enjoy. Take a deep breath. Relax and
take in the abundance of life.

Anonymous

Enjoy every
gift the world
has to offer.

I have a heart with room for every joy.

Philip James Bailey

If you want to feel rich, just count all
the gifts you have that money cannot buy.

Proverb

Abundance is not something we acquire.
It is something we tune into.

Wayne Dyer

Celebrate what
lifts you up.

One of the sanest, surest, and most encompassing joys of life comes from being happy over the good works and good fortune of others.

Archibald Rutledge

Some people make the world
more special just by being in it.

Kelly Ann Rothaus

Let us be grateful to people who
make us happy, they are the charming
gardeners who make our souls blossom.

Marcel Proust

Delight in
shared happiness.

All the really great things in life are expressed in the simplest words: friends and family; purpose and meaning; love and work; caring and community; appreciation and gratitude.

Dan Zadra

...life itself is a gift. It's a compliment just being born: to feel, breathe, think, play, dance, sing, work, and make love, for this particular lifetime.

Daphne Rose Kingma

The more you praise and celebrate your life,
the more there is in life to celebrate.

Oprah Winfrey

Appreciate small
miracles and
big wonders.

Every single day, do something
that makes your heart sing.

Marcia Wieder

Joy is what happens when we allow ourselves
to recognize how good things are.

Marianne Williamson

Remember that feeling as a child when
you woke up and the morning smiled?
It's time you felt like that again.

"Take a Giant Step," 1966

Invite joy in and
let it stay awhile.

Happiness is itself a kind of gratitude.

Joseph Wood Krutch

It's all yours.

COMPENDIUM®

live inspired

Written by and Compiled by: Dan Zadra and Kristel Wills

Designed by: Jessica Phoenix

Edited by: Kristin Eade

Library of Congress Control Number: 2019948086 | ISBN: 978-1-970147-04-9

1st printing. Printed in China with soy inks on FSC®-Mix certified paper.

Create meaningful moments with gifts that inspire.

CONNECT WITH US

live-inspired.com | sayhello@compendiuminc.com

@compendiumliveinspired
#compendiumliveinspired